Usborne
First Dot-to-Dot
Pirates

Join each group of dots to find
out what the pictures show, then
add a name sticker to each page.

Designed and illustrated by

Katrina Fearn

What do all the pirates sail in?

1 2 3 4 5 6 7 8 9 10

Molly the deckhand

1 2 3 4 5 6 7 8 9 10

Who's in charge of the pirate ship?

Polly the parrot

Who is climbing above the ship?

Treasure chest

1 2 3 4 5 6 7 8 9 10

Who has feathers and a big beak?

Pirate Percy

1   2   3   4   5   6   7   8   9   10

Who is scrubbing the deck of the ship?

Billy the lookout

1 2 3 4 5 6 7 8 9 10

Who likes eating tasty fish?

Sniffy the rat

Who has lots of very sharp teeth?

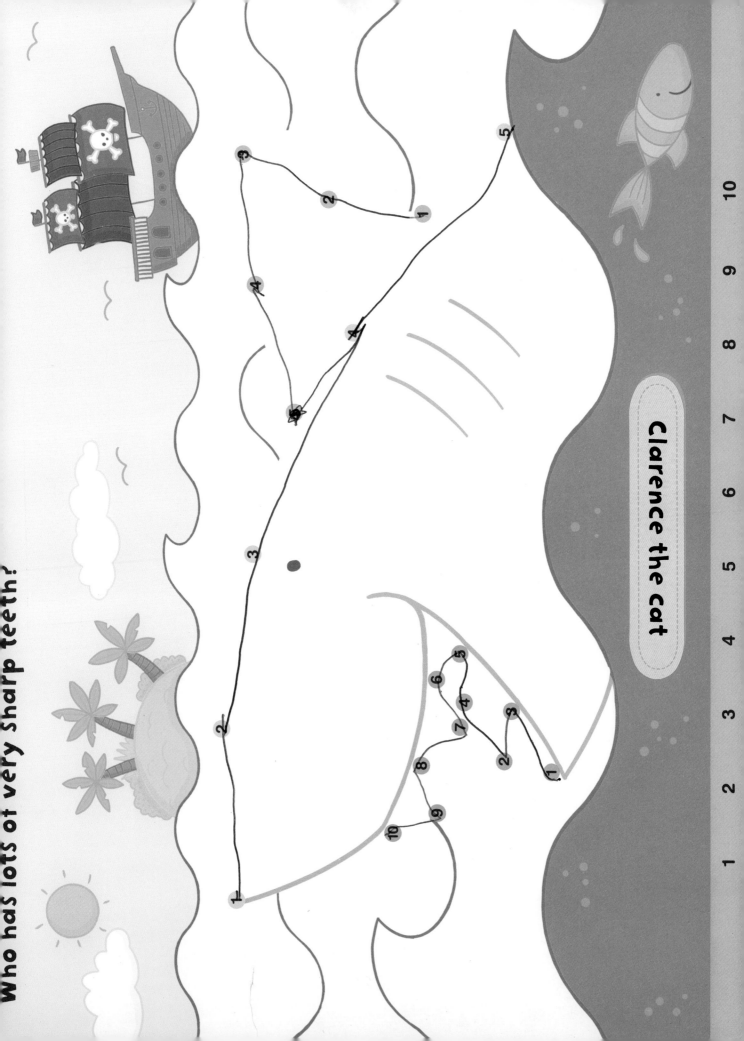

Clarence the cat

1 2 3 4 5 6 7 8 9 10

Who plays the violin?

Pirate ship

1 2 3 4 5 6 7 8 9 10

Who is dancing a pirate jig?

Pirate Jack

1   2   3   4   5   6   7   8   9   10

Who sneaks around the ship stealing food?

Captain Crayfish

Where do the pirates search for treasure?

Hungry shark

1 2 3 4 5 6 7 8 9 10

Who is holding a treasure map?

Pirate Bob

1 2 3 4 5 6 7 8 9 10

Who is looking for land?

Pegleg Pete

1   2   3   4   5   6   7   8   9   10

What has the captain found?

Desert island